SHADOWS
OF THE FUTURE

PROPHECIES FOR
THE MILLENNIUM

by
BILLY ROBERTS

CON-PSY PUBLICATIONS MIDDLESEX

First Edition

© Billy Roberts
1998

Published by

CON-PSY PUBLICATIONS

P.O. BOX 14,
GREENFORD,
MIDDLESEX, UB6 0UF.

Cover design by Carolyn James

ISBN 1 898680 12 4

SHADOWS OF THE FUTURE
PROPHECIES FOR THE MILLENNIUM

INTRODUCTION

Tall Pine is my Spirit Guide and Mentor. My association with him goes back into my childhood, in fact to my earliest days. At that time he appeared as solid and substantial to my young eyes as did my parents and family.

Tall Pine has always been a great source of strength and inspiration to me. He has guided me through some of the most traumatic periods of my life, and at times has been my only source of comfort and encouragement.

There have been occasions in the past when I thought and feared that he was merely a figment of my imagination - that he was just someone I had created in my own mind, out of a pressing need to be cared for. However, any doubts I have ever had regarding his existence have always been dispelled by his overwhelming personality and presence.

Tall Pine is of course a Spirit person - a discarnate being. In the mid nineteenth century he lived his life as a member of one of the numerous Indian tribes on the north American continent. However, his extreme sensitivity and profound spiritual beliefs made it very difficult for Tall Pine to blend with his contemporaries and their lifestyle .... He refused to fight, and he could not bring himself to kill animals.

At the age of seventeen Tall Pine was banished from his tribe. Wandering far away from the plains he chose to live out his life in total isolation in the mountains, alone with Nature. His physical life came to an abrupt end at the age of thirty two when, in attempting to prevent the slaughter of a bear by a group of hunters, Tall Pine was murdered.

Today Tall Pine is the leader of a group of Spiritual Teachers called THE ELDERS. He often refers to himself as being a facet of a diamond, that is, an aspect of the One, as in fact we all are. Although Tall Pine uses the diamond as a symbolic reference to God and the whole of Creation, I personally like to think of the group of ELDERS as a diamond, with they and myself as facets of it.

Tall Pine has been channelling Spiritual teachings through me for more than twenty five years. Although the teachings come through Tall Pine they are not his alone, for he is the appointed channel, and the one who represents THE ELDERS.

Here he answers some questions pertinent to the approaching Millennium, and channels some relevant Spiritual teachings. However, as this book is principally concerned with the fate of Planet Earth and those who live upon her, in the following pages Tall Pine makes a series of startling and sometimes frightening prophecies concerning the future of the Planet and unfolding World events.

4

It would appear that from the very beginning of recorded time traditions of a secret knowledge have been known which, because of the very nature of this knowledge, could only be passed on to those who could prove that they were ready and worthy to receive it. This they did by subjecting themselves to the most severe tests and trials.

This closely guarded knowledge was known, very generally, under the heading of 'THE MYSTERIES'. It was basically a core of teachings concerned primarily with the more profound aspects of man's being - his nature, origins, and relationship with Divine Beings, as well as of course with the evolution of the physical world and its natural laws.

There was nothing in any way speculative about this knowledge. On the contrary, it was in fact extremely powerful, and whoever acquired it also acquired the key, so to speak, to great mystical powers, which in turn gained them access to knowledge of THE FUTURE.

Many of the ancient Seers were in fact students of THE MYSTERIES. Some though fell from favour by prostituting themselves through misuse of the knowledge and powers they had acquired. The faithful and the loyal, however, were driven further into obscurity, fearing that they would be betrayed and forced to reveal those hidden truths that they themselves so carefully guarded - on occasion with their lives.

Over the last thousand years or so some of these secret teachings have filtered through, and having been translated in a way that the ordinary student of the subject could comprehend, they may often be found written down in books under the title 'THE LESSER MYSTERIES'. 'THE GREATER MYSTERIES' have never been seen in print, for these can only be passed on from teacher to pupil.

There was never any question of deceiving one's way into initiation. This could simply not be done, for when the student was ready the teacher would always appear. Nor was it always necessary to receive this knowledge verbally, for as with most Esoteric knowledge it arises from within, that is to say, it is Spiritually discerned by the Spiritual Mind of man.

And so today we are standing on the threshold of a Spiritual Epoch, the coming of which has been foretold by Seers for thousands of years.

The approaching Golden Age of the Millennium will give birth to a whole new concept of Spirit, which will eventually give rise in its turn to the expansion of man's consciousness towards God and Peace.

Many strange and wondrous manifestations will be witnessed over the next two hundred years. The children born in that time will possess and exhibit strange powers, the like of which have never before been seen. They will perform amazing feats - in fact the gadgets and gimmicks of the Mystics and Seers of today shall truly be the toys of your children tomorrow.

TIME is one of those great mysteries that man refuses even to try and comprehend. To enable him to live with it he has arbitrarily divided it into a past, a present, and a future. Those things he has already experienced he compartmentalises easily into the section of the past, but he seemingly has great difficulty in dealing with the present, at least until that too is ready to move into the past. He has no problem at all in recalling the past to the present, but what of the looming shadows of THE FUTURE?

Man would seem to perceive the future rather like a blind man wandering alone in some strange, mysterious land. He is afraid to gaze into the eyes of the future, or to listen to its words, for fear that the reality of who he truly is will dawn upon him.

BUT THE FUTURE HOLDS NO SECRETS. It wishes to tell those who would listen, and to reveal all to those who would look.

*****

Much of what the ancient Prophets 'saw' for the twenty first century and beyond is quite depressing, and even frightening. Some of the prophetic revelations in this book may in fact contradict what you have read in books written by ancient Seers, or in modern day interpretations of their works. A great many of the events they prophesied for the twentieth century and before simply did not occur. Perhaps their prophecies were misinterpreted, or maybe the true meaning was lost when they were deciphered.

I can of course hear you say "Why should this book be any different?" Well, it IS different, in a number of ways. Most importantly perhaps, it is written simply, clearly, and concisely. There are no hidden metaphors or dual meanings. It was channelled through me by a group of discarnate minds who I have, over the years, come to know and trust. They are known to me as THE ELDERS.

In view of the fact that The Elders' conception of Time is rather different from our own it may well be that some of the dates in the following text are slightly out, a notable example being the 'Diana Princess of Wales Prophecy'.

The Elders seem somewhat amused in fact by my continual insistence on the accuracy of dates.

"Your Time is not important" they say "It is the event itself which matters".

CHAPTER ONE

WORLD CLIMATIC CHANGES AND NATURAL DISASTERS

It would seem appropriate to begin a book such as this by looking at a subject which cannot fail to affect every living creature on this Planet, whether they be human, or members of the noble animal and plant kingdoms. I mean, of course, the climate.

We are in many ways at the mercy of our climate, for it is one of the few things which we simply cannot bend, affect, or change in any significant way in our favour. We are helpless in the face of the awesome might of a hurricane, and what else can we do but pray for rain when the Heavens run dry?

The phrase 'Global Warming' has crept into our vocabulary over the past few years, bringing with it a heightened public awareness of the changes occurring in the climate around us. Scientific opinion appeared to teeter interminably on the fence, before falling heavily down onto the 'changing climate' side.

So now it is official. We do not even need the evidence of the melting polar ice caps to tell us that our global climate is changing.

For those familiar with the works of the ancient Seers and Prophets this should come as no surprise. Nostradamus was but one among many to predict great climatic changes around the Millennium. In more modern times (1934) Edgar Cayce made a series of predictions about climatic changes and associated dramatic natural catastrophes, which he prophesied were to occur at the very end of the twentieth century.

The Elders too predict dramatic changes in our global climate, accompanied by severe, destructive natural catastrophes. These changes have already begun, and the Elders tell us that from the year 1999 onwards there will be a grave deterioration in the Earth's climate.

1999 will see the rapid acceleration of Global Warming until, by the year 2010, both polar ice caps will be gravely affected, sending flood waters rising rapidly all over the world. The effects will be devastating. Vast areas of low lying land throughout the globe, coastal areas and the cities on them, will begin to disappear into the sea.

I am not speaking now of events that will occur at some far flung future time. This is not a book of predictions relating to some comfortably far off epoch, glimpsed only dimly through the mists of time which divide it from us. Indeed not. For these climatic changes and their accompanying disastrous consequences are upon us now.

The race has begun. The first few steps have already been taken.

By the year 2010 there will be very little of Venice left above water. Sicily, and Italy too, will be seriously affected by then, as the rising sea level reclaims vast parts of their coastlines.

Throughout the first 100 years of the Millennium sea levels will continue to rise dramatically all over the world.

Japan will suffer greatly and, inevitably fighting a losing battle, much of that country will have been inundated, and will disappear completely, within the next 200 years.

It is interesting to note that Edgar Cayce also foresaw the loss of much of Japan, but at an earlier date than that given by the Elders. According to Cayce not only Japan, but great areas of Northern Europe, including Southern England, will vanish beneath the rapidly rising waters in or around the year 2000.

Within the next twelve years the inhabitants of Australia will see their climate begin to change dramatically. Accompanying this change will come great catastrophes such as hurricanes, and enormously destructive tidal waves. Severe flooding will devastate parts of the country.

A movement of the Australian population will begin, away from endangered coastal regions, towards the relative safety of inland areas. But the changing climate will devastate Australia's farm produce and wine production capacity, causing great hardship in that country.

The continent of Africa will begin to suffer greatly 40 years into the Millennium as a result of climatic changes. Floods will destroy habitations and food supplies, and devastating winds will lay waste the countryside. Many people will die as a result.

Egypt will be particularly badly hit 70 years into the Millennium. Freak gale force winds will cause shifting sands, and some cities will become almost uninhabitable as a result. Fierce rains, the like of which Egypt has never seen before, will compound the misery of those made homeless as a result of changing weather patterns.

Only a few years into the Millennium governments of countries with low lying coastal areas will be working to reinforce their sea defences. But the rise in tidal waters will be relentless, as Global Warming continues, and most of these sea defences will simply crumble and disappear below the invading waters.

As the climate around the world changes we will see today's warm countries becoming much colder, and the colder countries will find their climates becoming very much warmer. As this takes place, accelerating from 1999 onwards, earthquakes, volcanic eruptions, and flooding will occur all over the planet.

In Britain the climate will gradually be transformed until, 50 years

8

into the Millennium, we will live in an extremely pleasant, Mediterranean-like climate.

50 years after that, by the year 2100, Britain will be much warmer, and more pleasant climatically, than the continent of Europe. So much so, in fact, that Britain will have become a desirable place to live, and people from all over the world will be beating a path to these Isles. The wet, cold, windy and unreliable weather for which Britain has become notorious will be a thing of the past.

Many of the smaller islands which now surround the British Isles will have diminished greatly in size by the year 2250, and by 2500 virtually no trace will remain of Jersey, Guernsey , and the Isle of Man. In fact practically nothing of ANY of today's existing islands will remain above sea level by then.

Although Britain will have a warm and pleasant climate by the year 2100 there will be a price to pay. For the inhabitants will have to contend with fierce, torrential rains which will regularly cause flooding and loss of life.

The coastline of the United Kingdom will alter dramatically, as low lying areas are systematically submerged beneath the ever rising seas. This process has, of course, already begun, and will accelerate from 1999 onwards. Although Edgar Cayce predicts that London will be a coastal town as early as the year 2000 the Elders, although agreeing in principle, contend that it will take a little longer. However, Britain WILL gradually diminish in size, and little by little will be reclaimed by the rising waters.

By the year 2350 Britain will have shrunk so much in size that the vast majority of its inhabitants will have fled its shores to set up home in foreign countries.

*****

Shortly after the beginning of the Millennium, probably in the year 2003, Mount Etna will erupt violently. This will be the volcano's worst eruption ever. Not long after Mount Etna, Mount Vesuvius will also erupt, but will settle down again fairly shortly afterwards. However, only twelve months later Vesuvius will erupt again and this time the eruption will be extremely strong and destructive.

*****

In the year 2013 a frightening discovery will be made. Enormous cracks will have appeared in the surface of the Earth. Scientists and geolo-

9

gists from all over the world will examine these deep cracks using scientific probes, and they will reach the worrying conclusion that the cracks, which will have appeared in strategic areas, forming a kind of pattern over the surface of the Earth, have been caused by Global Warming.

Following this unwelcome discovery an international conference will be called as a matter of urgency. At this conference world leaders will unite and agree to take joint action to try to safeguard the Planet by preventing further climatic and global deterioration.

' This agreement will mark the first time that any real action has been taken to try to stem the alarming deterioration in the global climate. It will of course have been brought about out of fear for the Earth's future, and by implication, the future of mankind.

*****

The year 2013 will also mark the beginning of a series of natural phenomena such as earthquakes, (many of which will cause massive tidal waves), volcanic eruptions, floods and land slips. These natural disasters will be seen occurring all over the planet.

Australia will be hit by a series of fierce earthquakes, and hurricanes will devastate parts of South America.

In 2140 a volcano long thought to be dormant will suddenly erupt violently, without warning, on one of the Japanese Islands.. By this year the rising sea waters will have made such incursions into the islands of Japan that they will no longer resemble the islands of today. They will of course be much smaller in area, and many of today's large cities will already have vanished. The volcanic eruption will cause such enormous devastation and loss of life in that heavily populated area that Japan will never recover from the disaster.

*****

In 2200 the earthquake that everyone has been 'waiting for' will finally occur. San Francisco will be reduced to rubble by its worst earthquake ever. As the sledgehammer effect of the quake topples buildings and constructions, huge fires will break out as a result. The Fire Service will be helpless to respond, and thousands will die in the ensuing flames and destruction.

Many of the ancient Seers and Prophets have predicted such flames and destruction as a result of naturally occurring disasters around the turn of the century, or at the end of the world. Nostradamus speaks of a

10

'worldwide conflagration', and tells us that 'scarcely any lands will not be covered by water' at that time. He may in fact be interpreted as predicting specific earthquakes for parts of Europe, and also as indicating the sinking below the surface of the sea of part of England.

The shifts and movements of the Earth's crust will be responsible for the emergence of 'new' land masses from the sea, and 100 years into the Millennium several 'new' islands will appear above the surface of the Atlantic Ocean and of the Mediterranean Sea. These islands will be habitable, and will be gratefully colonised by groups of displaced people whose homelands have sunk beneath the rising sea waters.

Within 500 years of the start of the Millennium many of today's large countries will have diminished greatly in size. Their coastlines will have been eaten away, and will have crumbled into the sea. By this time Australia will have suffered enormously, and will have deteriorated and decayed, being greatly reduced in size, and having become but a poor shadow of the Australia of today.

However, some of today's smaller countries and islands, which one would expect to have vanished completely shortly into the Millennium, will in fact have grown in size, having reclaimed land from the surrounding waters.

Inevitably, when the full gravity of the effects of Global Warming on the World's climate, and thence on the World's land masses is realised, government will blame government, and bitter recriminations will fly from one side of the Earth to the other.

The Elders have something of interest to say about this. According to them, the phenomenon of Global Warming is a natural process which, they say, would have happened anyway, regardless of how we had treated the Planet, or what steps we had taken to prevent the build up of atmospheric pollution. The outcome of the process of Global Warming cannot therefore be avoided in any way. It is inevitable.

One can therefore only assume from what the Elders say that ultimately, one day, the complete demise of our Planet will come about.

CHAPTER TWO

WORLD EVENTS

War and aggression will be rife throughout the world during the first ten years of the twenty first century. It will almost seem as though there is conflict in every corner of the globe, and few regions will remain uninvolved in one way or another.

THE USA AND RUSSIA

In the year 2000 some very constructive talks will take place between the United States of America and Russia.

These talks will concern tests which Russia will be planning to carry out on a newly developed missile.

Following a short period of anxiety as the world awaits the outcome of the talks, a satisfactory agreement will be reached between the two countries. The tests will be postponed, to be recommenced jointly at a later date. ,

IRAQ

The new century will only just have begun when internal conflicts become apparent in Iraq.

The Iraqi leadership will make threats towards the USA, and will appear to be preparing their armies for war.

The eyes of the world will turn anxiously towards Iraq, wondering just what is going to happen.

In the year 2001 a prominent Middle Eastern figure, possibly a King, will be assassinated. Speculation and accusations will abound regarding the murder, and a major incident will break out in the area of Iraq as a direct result.

Initially Iraq, Iran and the USA will be involved in the contretemps, but Britain, France, and Israel will also become embroiled as the situation worsens.

Quite unexpectedly, in the midst of all this strife and turmoil, a virtually unknown British politician will emerge as an envoy of peace. He will travel to the Middle East, accompanied by a well known American diplomat. The two will be well thought of by all sides involved in the fighting, and thanks to their efforts progress will be made towards resolving the conflict.

However, it will be eighteen months before the war comes to an end. Thereafter there will be peace, albeit an uneasy peace, in the region for four years.

Not long after the resolution of this conflict the American diplomat involved in the peacemaking efforts will be killed tragically in a motoring accident.

RUSSIA

In the year 2001 a leading figure in the Russian government will die following an illness.

His death will plunge the country into a period of turmoil and strife, as a desperate political power struggle ensues.

Another leading political figure will be forced to resign suddenly, as a result of pressure brought to bear from within the Kremlin.

The world will wait anxiously to see where the balance of power will lie when the dust has settled.

By the year 2007 Russia will once again be labouring under Communist rule.

In that year dissent and internal conflict will break out in many parts of Russia. There will be fighting on the streets of Moscow, and the country will be plunged once again into turmoil.

Two strong political figures will be instrumental in governing Russia at this time. Only one of these men is known, and in fact in the public eye at this moment. The other will be an unknown quantity, and will seemingly emerge onto the political stage from nowhere. This unknown man will be strongly influenced by his wife, and they will both be extremely aggressive in outlook.

RUSSIA AND CHINA

Also in the year 2007 Russia and China will hold talks. As a result of these talks a new relationship will be formed between the two countries.

The Western powers will see this new relationship as a threat to their security, and the USA and Britain especially will become extremely anxious and suspicious of Russia and China's motives and intentions.

For a few years there will be some very tense situations, and a virtual return to the old cold war hostility between Russia and the West.

Russian troops will be stationed in the Far East, giving the West additional cause for concern.

The Russian leadership will make threats towards the USA, who will respond in a similar fashion.

This situation, which will develop into a kind of aggressive stand off between Russia and China on the one hand, and the Western powers on the other, will continue for quite a few years.

13

HONG KONG AND CHINA

The approaching hand over of Hong Kong to China will appear, on the surface, to go quite smoothly.

However, within three years of the hand over serious trouble will arise. The Chinese government will impose massive restrictions upon the people living in Hong Kong, and the way in which they may carry out their trading. This will cause enormous dissatisfaction and hardship for the people of Hong Kong.

China will flex her muscles and attempt to make her presence felt on the Western world. She will refuse to accept any criticism at all of her harsh treatment of the people of Hong Kong.

China's behaviour will eventually cause the USA to assert her authority, and although there will be serious friction for a time, and a great deal of worldwide anxiety, a possible major incident will be averted when other leading countries become involved in order to defuse the situation.

Nevertheless, for the next ten years China will appear restless and unpredictable, and will close herself totally once more to 'outsiders'. She will appear menacing, seeming to pose a major threat to the security of the western world.

FRANCE

In the year 2006 the young wife of a French politician will be kidnapped while on holiday in the South of France.

The kidnappers will demand a large ransom for her safe return, and this will be paid in full.

The politician's wife will be freed unhurt, but her kidnappers will never be caught.

In the year 2008 a terrorist bomb will explode in the centre of Paris. Two people will be killed. A small radical terrorist group will claim responsibility.

A few days later there will be a second bomb explosion, also in Paris. This time no one will be killed.

Shortly afterwards the French police will arrest a young black woman and a middle aged man at a farmhouse just outside Paris.

THE UNITED STATES OF AMERICA

The year 2002 will be an unhappy one for the USA.

Abroad there will seem to be aggression and conflict everywhere, and at home nothing will appear to be going right.

Early in 2002 will come the terrible news that an American plane carrying a full complement of passengers on board has crashed into the

14

ocean.

There will be no survivors.

Upon examination of the wreckage it will be discovered that a bomb was responsible for the disaster.

Amongst those who perish in the tragedy will be a popular American celebrity and his wife.

Later on in the same year a deranged gun man will go on the rampage in a shopping precinct in an American town.

He will fire indiscriminately at innocent passers by, killing fifteen and wounding many more.

Police will be forced to gun him down to prevent more deaths.

This horrific event appears to precipitate other copy-cat massacres in the USA.

The year 2002 will see the launch of another American space craft. Sadly, this one will go drastically wrong, and the craft will explode on take off.

ISRAEL AND PALESTINE

In the year 2001 a young Palestinian mother will be killed accidentally.

This incident will precipitate renewed trouble between Israel and Palestine, despite all the efforts of the Israeli government to promote peace.

There will be a great deal of fighting on the streets and loss of life, and for a time the situation will be extremely tense.

INDIA

Three years into the Millennium internal discord and strife will explode in India, and the country will be plunged into turmoil.

The government will flounder, seemingly unable to restore order.

The world's major powers will jointly send help in order to resolve the situation.

However, in the midst of it all a mentally ill student will murder a well known female political figure.

The ensuing violence and turmoil will plunge India into further chaos.

Famine will strike the country at this time and thousands will die as a result of starvation or disease.

PLANE CRASH

Approximately three years into the Millennium a plane carrying a group of foreign business men will crash and disappear over the Andes.

There will be great concern and great sadness as a result of this tragedy.

One of the missing men will be a well known American figure.

EVEREST

In the same year (approximately 2003) a well known and popular celebrity and entrepreneur will attempt to climb, or in some way to surmount, Everest (or a well known range of mountains).

However, there will be great national sadness when he is killed in the attempt.

FILMS

The year 2003 will be a sad one for the world of films. The industry will lose two well known celebrities.

The death of one, a veteran movie star from the late 1940s and 50s, will not be entirely unexpected.

But a much more recent movie idol will also die, this one killed tragically in an accident.

The film world will mourn their passing.

WORLD WATER SPEED RECORD

In the year 2003 the World Water Speed Record will be broken by a Dutch man.

He will have built the craft himself.

BRITAIN

In the year 2007 a strong charismatic woman will emerge onto the world's stage, coming seemingly 'from nowhere'.

In a voice which no one will fail to hear and heed, she will speak for the Animal Kingdom.

She will be their much needed champion, not only in Britain, but abroad too.

Such will be her power and influence that eventually an Animal Rights Party will be formed around her, and its influence will extend across the world.

MURDERS

The year 2001 will see the beginning of a deterioration in the spiritual and moral structure of today's society.

A great deal of evil and aggression will be seen throughout the world at this time, permeating every walk of life.

2001 will truly be 'THE DEVIL'S YEAR', with some of the most gruesome murders ever known emerging in Britain, the USA, France and Australia.

Two to four years into the Millennium a series of the most horrific murders will be brought to light. These murders will have been carried out by a woman and a young man. The pair will be arrested, and the whole world will be horrified when the truth is finally revealed.

They will have been committing murder for the past four years, and will have been responsible for the dreadful deaths of more than forty young people.

KILLER DISEASES

Within five years of the beginning of the new Millennium a hitherto unknown killer disease will emerge.

This new disease will take two forms and will attack the human brain, and the body's mobility.

Thousands of people will die as a result of this strange disease, which will defy all the experts' efforts to find a cure for it.

Gradually, however, it will disappear of its own accord, without a cure ever having been found.

Ten years into the Millennium more new killer diseases will emerge.

Science will establish that these diseases are in fact only one principal disease, manifesting in different forms.

These new diseases will have the effect of reducing the body's resistance, thereby making it more susceptible to serious infections such as pneumonia and chronic lung disease, as well as weakening the heart, lungs and respiratory system.

There will be world wide pandemonium and governmental concern when it emerges that these diseases are connected to meat eating.

Also during the first ten years of the Millennium ancient diseases, diseases long since thought to have been eradicated from the world, will re emerge with a vengeance throughout the globe, affecting not only the vulnerable poorer regions of the world, but also the industrialised Western nations.

Within twelve years of the start of the Millennium the whole world, East and West alike, will be ravaged by a new disease closely resembling one that has not been seen anywhere in the world for hundreds of years.

Thousands will die from this terrible disease while medical experts worldwide work flat out to find a method of treating it.

Some two years later a cure will finally be discovered.

Sixty years into the Millennium a frightening new development will make the headlines across the world. A strange and hitherto unknown disease will attack and destroy not just one or two species of tree, but it will ravage every kind.

It will begin to spread into the plant kingdom too.

This terrible disease will be known as 'THE BLACK DREAD', and it will threaten the very existence of all forms of vegetation upon the Planet.

Botanists from all over the world will be gravely concerned, and they will come together in a desperate attempt to discover a cure.

The disease will have started somewhere in the forests of Germany and Austria, but apart from this piece of information, little else will be known about it.

The disease will be indicative of a grave deterioration in the Earth's climate.

Enormous numbers of trees and plants will be killed off, and whole species will become extinct. Despite the best efforts of the world's greatest scientific minds no cure will be found for The Black Dread. So there will be enormous relief around the globe when, within five years, the disease dies away of its own accord.

Several species of tree and plant life will have been lost to the world forever. However, new species will be evolved through scientific means.

KUWAIT

Sixty years into the Millennium a child King will ascend the throne of Kuwait.

He will be no more than fourteen years old at the time of his accession, and thereafter will see his country through troubled times.

A young woman (not his mother) will stand at the right hand of the young King, and guide him wisely. She will teach him the art of being just and kind.

The young King will grow up to be a mighty King, possessing vision and a strong sense of justice.

The leaders of many Arab countries will watch him in anger, considering him to be a thorn in their sides.

In his fiftieth year this King will be gunned down and killed, in a garden which overlooks an orchard.

His assassination will precipitate a vicious and bloody battle, and will turn men against their fellow countrymen. The fighting will rage for at

18

least twelve months, and will finally cease with the intervention of a Western government.

AVATARS AND THE ANTI CHRIST

Reference is made in the writings of the majority of ancient and modern day Seers to the advent of an Avatar.

Similarly, the arrival of the Anti Christ, the 'Beast' of the Apocalypse of St John, is predicted by most Seers.

There is, however, little agreement on dates concerning the arrival on Earth of either the Avatar or the Anti Christ, although Nostradamus seems to tell us to expect the Anti Christ in the year 1999, following a total eclipse of the sun.

The Elders, though, prophecy the emergence of an Avatar - one who will guide the world into enlightenment - twenty to twenty five years into the new Millennium.

This Spiritual or Enchristed One will emerge in central India, becoming known to the world just before great periods of disastrous drought and famine befall that country.

He will be capable of performing great mystical feats, and will be recognised and respected by leading religions all over the world. He will travel to many countries and speak widely on television and radio.

This man will change the Spiritual face of India, and exert great influence worldwide. He will touch the hearts of millions of people.

The Avatar will be tall in stature, possessing Western-like facial features, and the ability to speak many languages.

He will have no connection with the present day Avatar Sai Baba.

The Elders prophecy that India's Avatar will not be alone in his work. For, in the year 2025 another Enchristed One will be born, this time in the southern part of France.

And 2027 will herald the birth of a third Avatar, this one in the eastern part of Spain.

These three men will know of each other's existence, and although they will not be related to each other in any way, they will all be very similar in appearance.

They will be 'Masters', and their lives will be dedicated to good work, particularly amongst the sick and the poor.

Neither of the European Avatars will become widely known in the world until they have reached their early twenties. At that time they will journey to central India to seek out their Indian 'brother'.

The three will meet together only on that one occasion, but their meeting will be a memorable one, and will be of great importance to the

19

Spiritual status of the world.

Many thousands of people from all walks of life, all religions, and all corners of the globe will become followers of these men.

Many books will be written about their lives and works and the miracles they perform.

The Elders tell us that man must prepare himself and make ready to combat the evil which will manifest in the world in the year 2209.

This will be an extremely problematic year where world events are concerned, and it is at this point that the Anti Christ will re emerge .

This evil, cunning, scheming man will emerge as a leader of men and he will, for a time, do good work. He will gain the people's trust initially, but will then lead them into war, forcing them to turn against each other.

This man will appear in the area of present day Uganda, a region already familiar with tragic deprivation and want, and sadly, with great atrocities. But he will lead the people of this region into poverty worse than they have ever before known, and will cause them untold misery as he remains in power over quite a long period of time.

He, personally, will commit some of the most heinous atrocities the world has ever seen.

But notwithstanding this, he will receive the hand of friendship and alliance from other powerful world leaders who will support him, and even walk beside him into battle.

The Elders tell us that this man will have the look of all that we conceive the Devil to be.

He will be well guarded, and surrounded by a group of loyal followers who would lay down their lives for him. He will, they say, have a wolf by his side - reminiscent, perhaps, of that other, twentieth century Anti Christ.

THE END OF THE WORLD AND 1999

The end of the world, and particularly the way in which that dreadful event may come about, has always held a fascination for the Prophets and Seers, of whom at least one in every age has cried "The end is nigh!"

The Bible, its pages bursting with Apocalyptic writings and accounts of the Last Judgment, warns us to expect to find ourselves within the very jaws of Hell as the Anti Christ leads the world to destruction at the last hour.

As the Millennium creeps closer the threat of a worldwide conflagration which could destroy every living thing, even the very air we breathe, has settled uncomfortably into our consciousness.

The sneaking suspicion that the coming Millennium will mark the end of the world is no new thing. Looking back we can see the same fear manifested down the ages. Perhaps today though this fear has grown into more than just a nagging possibility, as we now possess the weapons to wipe out the Earth.

There has been an upsurge of interest recently in the works of the Seers. Dates, possible dates, and assumed dates upon which they predict the world will end, have been re examined and recalculated.

Interestingly enough, however, even Nostradamus that great and gloomy soothsayer, although predicting Apocalyptic events, and terrible destructive wars at the end of the century, does not tell us that the world will end then.

Instead he speaks of the advent of a Golden Age, and the survival of the Earth until 3797.

Aleister Crowley in his book of prophecies 'The Book of the Law', has been interpreted as giving 1997 as the date at which an outbreak of war in Europe will spread throughout Eastern Europe.

He tells us to expect war at the end of this century but adds that, rather than destroying the world, this will regenerate it.

Edgar Cayce predicts the advent of World War Three in the year 1999. However, this war will not, he says, bring about the end of the world, but it will instead be followed by the dawning of the New Age, and the Second Coming of Christ.

So what of Armageddon? Does the Apocalypse await us at the turn of the century?

The Elders themselves do not say that the dawning of the new Millennium will see the end of the world. However, they DO tell us that the grave climatic deterioration, which today has already begun, will accelerate in intensity throughout the globe from 1999 onwards.

They say also that 1999 will be a year of global disasters, and of outbreaks of serious aggression throughout, but not confined to, many of the Eastern regions of the world.

In fact 1999 will be a year of global fear as the threat of an outbreak of war, which could engulf the whole world, looms large and menacing.

The USA and Britain will assert their authority in a show of strength, in an endeavour to restore peace.

A collective sigh of relief will cross the world as their efforts are in fact successful.

21

GERMANY AND 1999

In 1999 the discord which has been simmering below the surface for some time will break out violently in Germany.

The trouble will be engineered and precipitated by a newly created political party called The Youth Party.

The Youth Party will cause havoc and strife all over Germany by inciting riots, particularly in schools, colleges and Universities. The violence will be such that a great many Universities will come under marshal rule.

Although the government will eventually regain control of the situation, no real solution will be found, and the seeds of discontent sown throughout Germany at this time will not die away, but will remain in bitterness in the hearts and minds of the German people.

Forty five years later those same seeds will blossom dangerously, fuelled by the advent of yet another political party.

The leader of this new, angry party will be a heavily set man, with a thick mane of black hair. He will wield a powerful, almost magnetic influence over the German younger generation, and his powerful oratorical abilities will be reminiscent of Adolf Hitler's.

The eyes of the world will once again turn anxiously towards Germany. The bitterness and aggression of the days of the Second World War will seemingly have returned to that country.

Violence will flare up and ethnic communities will be targeted. Many migrant workers will be killed. There will be riots in the streets of cities across Germany, and the army will be called out to restore order.

In the midst of this turmoil and aggression a well known German political figure will be assassinated when a bomb, planted in his car, explodes.

This potentially disastrous situation will eventually be brought under control, violence being met with violence.

However, this influential man and his political party will remain a threat to Germany's stability for the next six years.

WORLD WAR

It will be ninety years into the Millennium before that which the Old Testament Prophets foresaw, and which man has for so long dreaded, comes to pass.

An incursion into either China or Russia will ignite a flame which it will prove impossible to extinguish, and a disastrous World War will break out.

This war will begin in the region of China and Russia, and will see these two countries in alliance, fighting side by side.

As the horrific situation escalates the whole world will be plunged into a nightmare of mayhem, destruction and suffering, as country battles against country, and race against race.

Some small countries will be totally obliterated, never to be restored, their populations massacred, the pitiful survivors scattered to the four winds.

Other countries will be reduced to piles of rubble, their landscapes rendered unrecognisable, their cities razed to the ground.

During the conflict Britain will be invaded by a country which today is extremely insignificant.

For a time it will appear that the end of Great Britain as a nation has come, as she is subjected to the rule of the invading forces.

Just as it seems that man is on the brink of the complete annihilation of both himself and Planet Earth, a new 'COUNSEL OF WORLD LEADERS' will be established.

This new organisation, meeting amid chaos and turmoil, will finally bring an end to the worldwide conflagration.

Peace will be restored, and although the shocking memory of these dreadful events will live on, peace will remain throughout the world for two hundred years or more, during which time there will not be another worldwide war.

THE GOLDEN AGE OF SPIRIT

The ancient Seers and Prophets frequently make mention of the coming of a great Spiritual Epoch on the earth.

Tall Pine and the Elders speak of a 'Global Transformation' which will occur during the approaching Millennium. By this they mean the end of one phase in man's Spiritual evolution, and the beginning of another.

They do not speak of the 'End of the World', but instead tell us about the advent, in the approaching Millennium, of 'THE GOLDEN AGE OF SPIRIT'.

However, before this enlightened and peaceful epoch dawns across the Planet, the world must pass through great periods of turmoil and disaster.

There will be famine and drought, the like of which the modern world has never before experienced.

There will be uprisings by the populations of Eastern countries; the devastation of a global war; aggression will lead to fighting in many different regions of the world, and there will be an enormous increase in crime and violence of all kinds in the Western world.

23

Added to this there will be the devastation caused by great natural disasters occurring all over the world.

Nevertheless, notwithstanding the series of dreadful events which they have prophesied for the early part of the new Millennium, the Elders insist that this approaching Millennium WILL be a GOLDEN AGE, and an age of profound revelations.

They speak of the 1960s as having been an important Spiritual Epoch, and a sort of preparation period for the Golden Epoch that is to come.

The children who will be born in the first twenty years of the new Millennium will be extremely gifted, their knowledge and understanding being far in advance of their years. The fields of the Sciences, the Arts and Music will all benefit from an influx of bright and gifted youngsters just a few years into the Millennium.

Many Spiritually gifted children will also be born, possessing amazing psychic abilities, the like of which we have never seen.

But the Elders tell us to beware, for the Devil will also bring in his own during this period, and in fact never will so much evil have been seen exhibited by young people.

For the first forty years of the new Millennium Good will constantly combat Evil. Many young people, the ' Devil's Children', will seem to have been born into the world unable to tell the difference between good and evil, right and wrong.

CHAPTER THREE

THE UNITED KINGDOM

By the time the people of Great Britain welcome in the new Millennium the country will have adjusted to life under a Labour government. However, the inevitable teething problems experienced of course by any new government, but most especially by one which has not held power for so very long, will cause more than a few problems along the way.

By the year 2001 the new Labour government will be experiencing trouble within its ranks, and cracks will be appearing in its smooth public facade.

Underhanded activities connected to foreign countries will surface in a scandal, and two Cabinet Ministers will be expelled from the Government as a result of their involvement. The aftermath of this affair will see some dramatic changes in the Government.

But the Labour Party will not be the only one to suffer public humiliation as a result of scandals of one kind or another. In the year 2000 there will be a very significant reshuffle in the Conservative Party, also precipitated by some sort of scandal.

This event will in fact mark the beginning of a change to the face of politics as we know it today as British public opinion, aghast at this series of scandals, swings sharply against their elected representatives.

In fact, the first ten years of the Millennium will bring several scandals to light within Parliament as a whole.

Three significant Members of Parliament will be dismissed during this period as a direct result of their involvement in undesirable or unlawful activities of one kind or another.

Public pressure, fuelled by anger at the behaviour of many of their elected representatives, will precipitate governmental changes, and fundamental changes within the Conservative Party.

The present Labour Government will not be elected at the next General Election. However, a new broad coalition under the umbrella name of 'Conservatives' will be formed, and will gain office at the following General Election. This broad coalition will remain in office for quite a long time.

*****

An elderly politician, who is a well known and well respected political figure today, will die suddenly around the month of February 2000. His passing will be mourned across the political spectrum.

25

Fifty years into the Millennium British Political Parties will be united in the governing of the country. The party politics of today will be a thing of the past. As well as a Prime Minister there will be a 'GOVERNING COUNCIL' in authority over him. This Council will be responsible for making any important final decisions in the conduct of government.

*****

Sad to say, there is no end in sight to the terrible conflict in Northern Ireland. Throughout all the periods of peace in the world in the future, Ireland and Britain will never be permanently at peace.

No sooner will the joyful church bells have rung out across the country, welcoming in the new Millennium, than the sound of exploding bombs and gunfire will fill the air of Belfast.

Peace talks will take place in a secret location early in the year, but with no real hope of any success. While these talks are underway British troops will be moving into Northern Ireland.

This will be one of the IRA's worst and most destructive campaigns, during which mainland Britain will also be targeted.

Following this campaign of violence the IRA will dramatically reinforce its whole operating structure in response to British efforts to infiltrate its ranks.

In the year 2003, in a new campaign which will continue for twelve months, the IRA will again target major cities throughout the UK. However, four years into the Millennium a new political body will be formed in Northern Ireland, ushering in a brief respite in the violence.

A tall, charismatic figure will emerge to lead this new party, and the hopes of many will rest upon his shoulders. This man will eventually be instrumental in helping to restore a semblance of peace to Northern Ireland. However, before that day dawns there will be a seemingly never ending tide of fighting and bloodshed in that troubled land.

*****

I have mentioned previously that during the first forty years of the Millennium the world will see more evil, particularly exhibited by the young, than we have ever before experienced.

Already today we are hearing much about the 'breakdown' in the structure of our society. Crime of all kinds is escalating, and our existing police force would seem to be unable to stem the flow of the rising tide of wanton violence and lawbreaking.

Twenty to thirty years into the new Millennium this breakdown in our society will be so pronounced, our streets so unsafe, violent crime so widespread, that another force, a 'LAW AND ORDER FORCE', will by necessity be established to work alongside the existing police force on the streets of Britain's major cities.

But Britain will not be alone in experiencing such problems, and they will in fact be mirrored on the streets of the majority of large cities throughout the Western world at this time.

*****

In the year 2002 one of the worst winters ever to hit Britain will bring the country to a veritable standstill. There will be very heavy snowfalls, with deep drifting in most areas. These dreadful weather conditions will really take the country by surprise.

The worst of the snow will fall on Scotland and Yorkshire. Several people will be killed as a result of the sub zero temperatures when they are trapped in their cars. Others will die from accidents or heart attacks precipitated in one way or another by the severe weather. The whole country will be paralysed for several days by the snow and freezing temperatures.

In the following year, 2003, there will be a heat wave during the summer months, with the highest temperatures recorded for many years. This will cause problems of a different kind as the Water Authorities cast anxious eyes over the rapidly falling water levels in the country's reservoirs.

As I have already mentioned, the climate of the British Isles will eventually be transformed, becoming much warmer and almost Mediterranean-like by the early part of the new Millennium. This change has already begun and will accelerate rapidly from 1999 onwards.

But the climate is the determinant of our way of life, and of the very kind of life which evolves and exists in a given area. Thus, as the climate changes, becoming more 'Continentalised', so too will our native species of plants and animals.

The variety and type of insects will change too. Some which have never been seen in this country before will 'move in and settle here', so to speak. Inevitably, many insects will increase in size. I mention this particularly because the nation will be plagued by huge cockroaches and enormous spiders.

The higher temperatures will also attract, amongst other creatures new to these shores, several species of reptiles only ever seen in Equatorial climes.

The change in the climate here in Britain will inevitably precipitate changes in our life style. Working practices will alter. The heat will eventually mean that one will be required to work only in the mornings. In industry afternoon work will become optional, and will be paid at a higher rate.

One hundred years into the Millennium new forms of fruit and vegetables will have evolved as a result of the substantially warmer climate. Some of today's familiar trees and plants will have succumbed to the new conditions and died out, making way for new species better suited to such a climate.

The familiar British countryside as we know and love it today has but a limited time left. This 'green and pleasant land' is on the brink of enormous changes which will transform not only our countryside, but also our very way of life.

Two hundred years into the Millennium, with the waters around the globe still rising steadily, and coastal areas of Britain continuing to disappear beneath the relentless seas, architects will begin to design and build houses on stilts, particularly in vulnerable low lying areas. This form of habitation will prove popular, and 'stilt houses' will spring up across the country.

*****

Around the month of May in the year 2000 another new television channel will be tested. However, it will not go according to plan, and will encounter problem after problem.

*****

In the year 2002 or 2003 a scandal concerning a well known and much loved comedy celebrity will be rekindled. The star will be hounded by the press, and he will be made to feel that he has nowhere to run to and nowhere to hide.

Unable to cope with the unbearable pressure put upon him, he will commit suicide.

Amid great public sadness there is outrage at the treatment meted out to the star by the press, prior to his suicide.

A major national newspaper will subsequently be accused of his harassment.

In the year 2008 Manchester United will beat Arsenal in the Cup Final.

A horse called SIBERIAN SUMMER will win the Grand National in the same year, ridden by a hitherto unknown jockey named TOMMY RIMMER.

The year 2008 will in fact be a good year for sport, particularly Tennis, as an English man will become the Wimbledon Champion.

The only cloud on the British sporting horizon at this time will be the question, arising yet again, over the future of the Grand National. It will seem at one point as though the year 2008 will mark the end of the Grand National forever. However, it will eventually be decided that the race should continue, but bowing to public opinion, it will be altered drastically.

*****

Two hundred years into the Millennium the Government of Britain will invite representatives of armies from around the world to march together in friendship through the streets of London.

This festive occasion will be held to celebrate and promote peace throughout the world.

An army clad in green, black and grey will take part in the celebrations, and will march carrying Holly and Christmas berries.

This very same army will soon return to the shores of Britain, but this time as an enemy. There will be bitter fighting on the streets of London for two to three months, as this foreign power attempts to invade and take control of the country.

The eyes of the world will watch events but not intervene, as Britain fights to free herself from the threat of this mighty hand that has come to sweep the nation clean.

But free herself she will, in a matter of a very few months. However, it will take Britain more than three years to completely recover from this entirely unexpected ordeal. But recover she will, with the helping hands of many nations.

CHAPTER FOUR

THE ROYAL FAMILY

The first two years of the Millennium will see major changes within the Royal family. They, and the younger members in particular, have certainly been living through a difficult time over the past few years.

The bad publicity which certain members of the Royal Family have brought upon themselves has led, at least in part, to a sharp swing of public opinion against them. Some of their critics have been so fierce in their condemnation of the behaviour of the Royals that a new public debate has arisen of late: 'Is the dissolution of the Monarchy in sight?'

MEETING

Around mid November 1999 a special meeting will be held between the Queen and the Prime Minister.

The object of this meeting will be to discuss further plans for the future of the Royal Family.

The subject of the Queen's residences will be high on the agenda, as will be plans to dispose of other assets held by the Monarchy.

PRINCE CHARLES

November 1999 will be a problematic month in more ways than one for the Prince of Wales.

At that time Charles will be hounded by the media, as headlines dramatically declare that he is having a relationship with the daughter of an important public figure.

The Queen will instruct Charles to take a winter break, away from the constant attention of the news hounds. But he must take care. For his mind will be extremely unsettled at this time, and he may have a minor mishap whilst either climbing or skiing.

Such will be the media attention and public curiosity lavished on Prince Charles concerning his new romantic attachment, that this too will be a subject under discussion during the Queen's meeting with the Prime Minister.

THE DUCHESS OF YORK

Around the end of November 1999 the Duchess of York will find herself in yet more financial difficulties.

She will actually be threatened with court action, but will avoid it by the skin of her teeth when she manages to sign an extremely lucrative contract for a new book.

Recent rumours concerning a possible reconciliation between the Duke and Duchess of York have come to nothing, but by the year 2000 the couple will once again show signs of rekindling their relationship.

Media interest will be aroused and speculation will abound, but to the nation's disappointment nothing whatsoever will come of it.

PRINCESS MARGARET

Princess Margaret will be taken ill around December 1999.
She will enter hospital for tests and there will be a great deal of concern over her condition.

She will however make a full recovery, and will spend some time convalescing in Scotland.

DIANA

In the year 1999 Diana's personal life once again hits the headlines.

This time she will be linked romantically to a well known personality who is connected to the world of Theatre and Film.

He will be a wealthy, dark haired, foreign business man.

The intensity of the media coverage, both at home and abroad, will put a tremendous strain on the relationship.

Diana will eventually live between England, the USA and France, and it is in the latter country that she will meet her death tragically, in an automobile accident near water.

PRINCE CHARLES, THE MONARCHY AND MARRIAGE

Prince Charles will definitely never be crowned King.

He will go through all the motions and preparations and will declare himself ready to ascend the throne. However, public murmurings against the Prince will develop, two years into the Millennium, into angry public outcry and protestations against him.

The sheer weight of adverse public opinion will finally cause Charles to pay heed to his worried advisers, and he will step down, giving up his right to be crowned King.

Thereafter, angry and bitter and in some ways lost, Charles will immerse himself in business interests in Britain and abroad, spending much of his time travelling and avoiding the public gaze.

Although today there is a great deal of speculation regarding Charles' relationship with Camilla Parker Bowles, and whether or not it will end in their marriage, I have to say that it will not.

Charles will not marry Camilla, not because of any particular obstacle placed in their way, but simply because he will not want to.

The couple will remain good friends even though Camilla will remarry.

Charles himself will never remarry, but he will form an enduring romantic attachment to someone else.

THE ROYAL WATCHERS

Within the first two years of the Millennium journalistic sleuths working for a national newspaper will discover the existence of a body of 'ROYAL WATCHERS'.

This group will have been set up mainly to gather potentially harmful information about, and devise ways of discrediting the Royal Family.

Their aim will be to bring about the demise of the institution of the Monarchy.

The national newspaper will disclose the identities of the members of this group, and there will be public outcry and indignation as it is revealed that it is composed of politicians and journalists.

PRINCE EDWARD

Prince Edward's forthcoming marriage, although seemingly made in Heaven and set to last, will in fact endure for only four years, after which time there will be yet another Royal divorce.

Thereafter Prince Edward will make a successful career for himself in journalism and television, but always behind the scenes and away from the limelight.

In later years Prince Edward's name will be linked with some sort of scandal.

ABDICATION, PRINCE WILLIAM, PRINCE HARRY

We have heard much over the past few years on the subject of the possibility of the Queen's abdication.

However, the Queen will certainly NOT abdicate, and will in fact reign until her death at the age of ninety two.

She will have been widowed twelve years previously.

The first ten years of the Millennium will see the gradual dissolution of the Royal Family.

Like his father before him, Prince William will also never be crowned King. He will however serve as Monarch for a short time, but there will be so many fundamental changes going on in the structure of British politics and society at that time that he himself will choose not to be crowned.

But while Prince William will be the focus of public attention in the early years of the new Millennium, it is in fact Prince Harry, Charles and Diana's youngest son, who will excel and win the affections of the British people.

As he reaches adulthood Prince Harry will reveal his true character, and his great sensitivity, by becoming involved in the plight of the poor and impoverished both at home and abroad.

The young Prince will also exhibit an abiding love of animals, and will become involved in one way or another in the movement for the promotion of Animal Rights.

Prince Harry will marry a 'commoner', and all his life he will shun the bright lights and publicity which have been so much sought after by other members of his family.

He will travel extensively throughout the world, but his great love of nature and the Animal Kingdom will lead him to settle eventually in the rural peace and quiet of Scotland.

Prince Harry will most certainly be a 'Prince of the People', and will hold a special place in the affections of the British nation.

However his brother, Prince William, will not fare so well in this respect and will eventually reveal himself to be arrogant, self centred, and extremely materialistic. He will become unpopular, and will be disliked by the British public.

THE END OF THE MONARCHY

By the year 2050 the institution of the Monarchy will exist in name only.

There will be no reigning Monarch as Head of State, and no member of the Royal Family will retain a say, however small, in the running of the country.

Approximately seventy five years into the Millennium Great Britain will have reached an all time low. Crime of all kinds will have increased to levels never before experienced, and one of the consequences will be a drastic drop in tourism, and obviously in the revenue which that industry brings into the country.

At this time public opinion will begin to shift towards the idea of reinstating a Royal Head of State.

This idea will gain ground quickly, swelling into a movement with such a large and vocal following that the Government of the day will no longer be able to ignore the voice of the people.

In a bid to resolve the situation a referendum will be organised, in an attempt to accurately gauge public opinion.

To everyone's surprise however, the result of the referendum, when it comes, will show a majority AGAINST reinstating a Royal Head of State.

There will be an immediate public outcry, and accusations of poll tampering by a corrupt Government will be heard from many lips.

Feelings will run high throughout the whole country, and this public anger will lead to a scandal within Governmental bodies.

Despite this obvious public dissatisfaction, even when the dust has settled and calm has been restored, a Royal figurehead will still not be reinstated.

But the fiasco of the referendum result will continue to rankle in many quarters, and dissatisfaction with a system which could allow such corruption will abound.

For the following thirty years Britain will experience a period of strife and profound disharmony throughout society.

CHAPTER FIVE

STRANGE HAPPENINGS

A LOST CIVILISATION

Fifteen to twenty years into the new Millennium the attention of the whole world will be riveted on the amazing events unfolding in the Atlantic Ocean.

A strange phenomenon will occur in the waters of that Ocean, creating enormous, destructive tidal waves, which will cause severe flooding along Atlantic coastal regions.

As a result of this odd occurrence an incredible and yet strange discovery will be made within the waters of the Ocean itself.

There will be world wide excitement as the missing links to a long lost civilisation are revealed there.

A thrill of anticipation will hold mankind in awe as a city, lost to the world for countless ages, rises from its hidden resting place in the depths of the Ocean.

The sudden emergence from the depths of this wondrous city will stun scientist and layman alike, not the least because these missing links, so unexpectedly discovered, will reveal that visitors from another world have once had strong connections with this lost and long since forgotten civilisation.

This incredible discovery will cause scientists to rethink their existing theories about the origins of life on this Planet.

Although initially many people will be of the opinion that here at last is the lost civilisation of Atlantis, I have to say that this will NOT be the case. For the city which will break through the surface of the Atlantic Ocean, and rise into the light of day, will have been constructed at another time, by another civilisation.

COLLISION IN THE HEAVENS

In the first half of the twentieth century Immanuel Velikovsky published his book 'Worlds in Collision'. Drawing on information gleaned from the Bible and from the writings of ancient civilisations around the globe, Velikovsky contended that the Earth had been struck on at least two occasions in its past by a comet, causing momentous devastation.

The Elders tell us that there will be an enormous collision in the Heavens fifty years into the Millennium.

This shocking event will cause panic to sweep across the world, fuelled by the belief that the end of Planet Earth has come.

The collision, occurring so very close to the Earth, will not have been foreseen by the world's astronomers, and will therefore come as a severe shock to the entire population of the world.

Nothing like this will ever have been witnessed before, and it will certainly be a spectacular sight to behold.

Despite dire warnings from many quarters of ensuing doom and destruction, no one on Earth will be hurt, although many will thereafter catch their thoughts straying uneasily towards the extreme vulnerability of our Planet's situation in space.

This collision, which will be responsible for wonderful and highly visible manifestations in the space around our planet, will in fact precede many more strange and wondrous happenings, both in the Heavens and on the Earth.

Many unusual and extremely gifted children will be born from this time onwards, and the climate of the Earth, having already undergone substantial changes, will pass through a period of remarkable alteration and adjustment.

Animals which science had once thought to be extinct will be rediscovered, alive and thriving on the planet.

New stars will appear in the night sky, causing great excitement amongst the world's astronomers.

The appearance of these new stars will coincide with a strange alteration in the light which reaches and illumines our planet. At certain times of the year the daylight will be noticeably brighter and sharper than ever before, and the greatest scientific minds will not be able to agree upon the cause.

CHAPTER SIX

DISCOVERIES AND INVENTIONS

THE MEDICAL FIELD

Although the early years of the Millennium will see radical benefi-
cial advances in the medical field, with discoveries and inventions as yet
undreamed of, it will not be until the year 2005 that a cure for AIDS is
finally discovered.

In fact 2005 will see the discovery of not one but two different
methods of curing this terrible disease.

Medical researchers in Sweden and in the USA will be responsible
for the lifesaving discoveries, but France will also play a part.

In the same year, 2005, there will be another major breakthrough
in the field of medicine when American researchers discover a drug which
will slow down the effects of Multiple Sclerosis (MS). Two years later this
drug will be further developed and refined and will be responsible for bringing a great deal of relief to sufferers of MS.

*****

Five to seven years into the Millennium there will be a major
breakthrough in the treatment and easing of severe pain.

The sufferer will simply 'plug into' a small machine, and the pain
and discomfort will immediately be completely eliminated.

*****

Ten years into the Millennium will see another major medical
breakthrough, this time in the fight against cancer.

Cures will be discovered for several virulent types of cancer, and a
discovery will be made which will revolutionise the treatment of all kinds
of cancerous diseases.

At the same time a blood substitute will be discovered which will
completely eradicate Leukaemia, particularly in children.

*****

Shortly after these advances medical science will develop artificial
hearts and lungs.

There will be five years of testing and experimentation before these artificial organs are used successfully. When this happens the lives of countless thousands of heart and lung disease sufferers will be transformed.

It is interesting to note that fifteen years further on along the road of research and development in this field it will be impossible for those with transplanted lungs to drown. The possibilities here will be endless.

*****

Fifteen to twenty years into the Millennium great excitement will surround the discovery of a revolutionary device enabling visually handicapped people to see.

This wonderful invention will involve the implanting into the brain of the visually handicapped person of a sort of micro television.

The device will restore vision almost totally, even to those who have been blind from birth. However, in these latter cases, it will be necessary to implant a further micro instrument which I believe will be called an 'OPTICAL IMAGERY TRANSPOSER'.

*****

At about the same time new methods of treating mental diseases, particularly Schizophrenia, will prove remarkably successful.

*****

In the year 2010, or thereabouts, botanists will discover previously unknown plants in both Africa and Mexico.

Research will reveal that these plants possess amazing curative properties which will revolutionise the treatment of dermatological conditions and hitherto incurable diseases of the Pancreas and Liver.

Scientists will discover that the flower of one of these plants, which will be purple and white in colour, is useful in the treatment of diseases which affect the nervous system, particularly Multiple Sclerosis.

*****

Around the year 2025 the use of Solar Energy will extend into many areas of the home and workplace.

Amongst the more unusual uses of this energy will be the invention of a special kind of 'Solar Energised Corset' for the elderly.

By wearing this 'Corset' elderly people will find their mobility vastly improved, and their aches and pains will be eased.

In fact by the year 2025 the elderly will no longer have anything like as much difficulty moving around as they do today.

Thirty years into the Millennium the invention of a similar Solar powered garment will aid the recovery of those suffering spinal or leg injuries. This invention too will transform the lives of many.

*****

By the year 2035 science will have progressed greatly in the field of medicine.

The body scanning devices in use today will tomorrow be a thing of the past.

By 2035 it will be possible to obtain a patient's complete anatomical and physiological profile simply by connecting them up to a computerised 'PHYSIO-ANATOM PROFILER', as I believe it will then be called.

The PHYSIO-ANATOM PROFILER will inform the doctor of any malfunction anywhere in the body, and will also specify the correct treatment to be followed.

The diagnosis and prognosis will be printed out when the patient's profile has been completed.

*****

By the year 2040 further advances in the medical field will enable the human brain, its structure and circuit patterns, to be reproduced artificially, without in any way interfering with or altering the person's psychological status or make up.

In fact it will be possible to transform the whole psychology of a patient who has suffered from severe mental illness for many years, by means of a 'TRANSPOSER', the 'in' word at that time.

Using the same technique, that of 'TRANSPOSING', a person with an addictive personality, someone who has perhaps been addicted to either drugs or alcohol for many years, and who is finding it extremely difficult to deal with the habit, will have the option of being 'TRANSPOSED'.

In this way the addict will be completely cured, never to return to the addiction.

The 'TRANSPOSING' technique, as it is refined and adapted, will revolutionise all aspects of the medical field in the future, prolonging and enhancing the lives of many people.

Its use, quite obviously, will not be without controversy, and the public debate on the ethical and moral connotations of the use of the 'TRANSPOSING TECHNIQUE' will run and run.

*****

Around the year 2050 another exciting discovery will be made.

A strange and extremely unusual metal will be uncovered on the Equator.

This newly discovered metal will possess marvellous and mysterious properties, from which many new medicines will be derived. Nothing like it will ever have been seen before.

Research will also discover that this 'new' metal can be utilised as the source of a new energy which will subsequently be used in the fields of industry and medicine.

TIME TRAVEL

1999 will be a year of discoveries and inventions.

Amongst other things the concept of man's ability to travel through TIME will be seriously experimented with.

The possibilities thus discovered will be revealed to the world. However, the full extent and findings of these experiments will be withheld from the public until a future date, although it WILL be announced that man now has the knowledge to, and soon will, travel faster than the speed of light.

The experiments in this respect which will be revealed, will be shown to be successful.

GENETICS

At the same time, around the year 1999, discoveries will be made in the field of Genetics.

Although it will be in its innovative stages scientists will be on the verge of discovering a method by which a person's entire Genetic structure can be changed.

Prior to this, discoveries will have been made enabling scientists to isolate a specific gene, responsible for hereditary conditions.

But from now on research will leap from success to success, and discoveries will be made which will make it possible eventually to eradicate life threatening diseases completely.

This will not become a reality for a further twenty five years, but when it does, it will be a further step in the development of man's longevity.

40

POWER PACKS

By the year 2015 the popular science fiction of today's books and movies will have become a reality.

The POWER PACKS of science fiction with which we are all familiar, which are worn on the back enabling the wearer to be propelled into the air, will actually have been invented.

Although these Power Packs will be highly modified versions of the ones we have seen on the big screen, they will in fact be readily available in shops, and will be one of the main forms of travel in the future.

Twenty years later, by 2035, the traveller will undertake his journey enclosed in a sort of perspex bubble, rather similar to the Bubble Car of the 1950s and 60s.

Using this mode of transport the traveller of the future will be able to cover distances of up to two hundred miles, at a speed of seventy miles per hour.

THE GRAVITY NEUTRALISER

Around the year 2009 Sweden, having previously developed the 'GRAVITY NEUTRALISER', a device which alters the gravitational pull, thereby rendering objects almost weightless, will develop a greatly improved version of this device.

As well as offering the obvious benefits of weightlessness, it will also be adapted and refined in order to aid those with walking difficulties. In this field it will prove extremely useful.

THE CAR OF THE FUTURE

In the year 2004 a new, innovative, streamlined car will be exhibited at the Earls Court Car Show.

Enormous world wide excitement will surround the first public viewing of this car, as it will truly represent the car of the future.

The appearance of this car will mark the beginning of computerised motoring, and will provide more than an insight into what motoring will be like in the future.

The car will most probably be developed by Jaguar, and everything in it, from the air conditioning to the lights, will be completely computerised.

This amazing car will certainly whet the appetites of tomorrow's motorists, but they will probably have to wait another two to four years after the show to see it on the road.

Twenty five years into the Millennium, however, computerised cars will be common place in certain parts of the world.

Cars will eventually be programmed to reach their destinations, making the whole concept of travel on the roads much quicker and safer, by cutting out the need for human input.

*****

From the year 2020 most roads in vulnerable areas will be heated against severe frost, making travel in the wintertime much safer.

Forty to fifty years into the Millennium man will travel along the surface of a road without actually touching it.

THE PLANE OF THE FUTURE

In the year 2010 the USA will demonstrate a new American built Fighter plane.

The world will be awe struck - this plane will seem to have come straight out of the pages of a science fiction book.

It will be capable of far greater air speeds than any other plane on the market and, astonishingly, it will be capable of taking off from the Ocean bed, and moving through water at great speed.

The plane will have enormous fighting potential and a high safety factor, cutting down the risks of a fatal crash at sea.

This incredible plane will truly be an innovation, and will symbolise exactly what we can expect from the new Millennium.

TRAVEL AND TRANSPORT IN THE FUTURE

Just as the concept of television would have sounded completely impossible and bizarre one hundred and fifty years ago, so I am aware that the following prediction will sound equally far fetched and impossible to achieve.

Nevertheless, it is a fact that sixty years into the Millennium man will travel unseen.

For, as early as 2060, man will travel in some sort of 'TRAVEL SHIP', at such speeds as to make it invisible.

In the more distant future the great minds of science will discover a way of breaking down matter to such an extent that it will be possible for man himself to become invisible. This will not become a reality however, until at least one hundred and twenty years into the Millennium.

For the adventurous, recreational journeys to the Moon are not as far off as one might imagine. In the true spirit of science fiction a trip to the Moon will be a real possibility just ninety five years into the Millennium.

At this time however, the journey and mode of travel will be in its innovative stages, so a return trip will be very expensive and within the reach of only the very wealthy.

The first few craft on the 'Moon Run' will seat only ten people, but there will be no shortage of those ready and willing to pay for the privilege of journeying at their own peril.

THE TELEVISION OF THE FUTURE

Twenty years into the Millennium will prove to be an exciting time for the housewife and for the elderly, who will find a cluster of new inventions making their lives easier as time goes by.

As early as ten years into the Millennium our televisions will be linked up to the telephone, enabling us to see, if we wish, the person to whom we are speaking.

Television will be revolutionised. Home television will become vitally important, and in many ways life in the future will revolve around it.

The television screens of today will become obsolete, being replaced by Solar powered computer chips which will be inserted into the living room wall. When activated they will produce a large picture of astounding clarity across the wall.

When deactivated there will be no trace of any television, and only the room's decor will be visible.

Trips to the supermarket, the stuff of nightmares for many of today's elderly, will quickly become a thing of the past.

Special TV shopping channels will be established, enabling one to flick through them, rather like flicking through the pages of a catalogue.

Everything imaginable will be available from TV supermarkets and TV specialist stores, from Sunday lunch to soap powder, and from the very latest clothes to foreign holidays.

All the potential customer will need to do will be to make a simple telephone call and their order will be delivered within the hour.

Stiff competition between these TV stores will see to it that their standards will remain high, and TV shopping will swiftly enter our way of life and remain there.

Certain channels will be linked up to Doctors, enabling consultations to take place through the TV and telephone.

This innovation in particular will assume great importance not only in the case of medical emergencies, but for the elderly and housebound, for whom medical help and advice will henceforth always be available via the television.

SOLAR ENERGY

Twenty five years into the Millennium the majority of homes will be Solar energised.

Domestic power as we know it today will be a thing of the past.

Uses will be found for Solar energy in many different spheres of life. For example some packs of food which will require no cooking will be on sale. One will simply peel off a Solar strip, and the Solar energy will interact with a specially prepared container to effect a self cooking process. Within minutes the contents will be cooked and ready to eat.

Picnics will be a pleasure - no more struggling to light a damp stove.

And of course for the elderly and the convalescent there will always be an effortless cooked meal on hand.

THE WARFARE OF THE FUTURE

In the year 2017 warfare will take on a completely different and sinister new meaning.

In that year Russia will reveal a new weapon which she will have been working to develop for some years.

The 'ULTRASONIC NEUTRALISER' will shock the world.

A high powered computer-like machine, it will be capable of producing and discharging Ultrasonic Neutralising Rays. These invisible rays will be able to travel any distance around the globe, homing in with astounding accuracy on opposing forces, and rendering them literally helpless, either permanently or temporarily.

The ULTRASONIC NEUTRALISER will be capable of either killing or temporarily immobilising any enemy, either collectively or individually.

Although initially developed by Russia, this horrific weapon of war will be taken up and further developed and refined by the USA.

PSYCHIC SCIENCE

Traditional and Psychic science will not actually manage to work hand in hand until at least twenty five years into the Millennium.

At this time the existence of a Spirit World will be scientifically discovered, although this wonderful discovery will not be disclosed to the general public for a further ten years.

Even at that time the full facts as they will then be known will not be revealed.

A television-like monitor which will enable a two way conversation to take place between the living of this world and the 'dead' of the

Spirit World, will eventually become a reality.

Using what will be called 'TRANS - VIBRATORY MODULA-TORS' scientists will be able to receive clear pictures and sound from the world of the so called 'dead'.

Enormous excitement and interest will inevitably surround the development of these TRANS - VIBRATORY MODULATORS, but it will be a further seventy years or more before this revolutionary technique is actually seen on the market.

AIR TRAVEL OF THE FUTURE

The Age of Aquarius will give rise to some extremely significant developments where aircraft are concerned.

Early in the Millennium the mode of travel from one side of the Atlantic Ocean to the other will become much quicker and more comfortable.

Two hundred years into the Millennium aircraft will have evolved to such an extent that they will then be able to accommodate three thousand people comfortably on long haul trips.

These enormous craft will contain everything imaginable, and will be geared towards the comfort of the traveller of the future.

On board will be:

Night clubs; ballrooms; cinemas; beauty parlours; shops of all descriptions selling all manner of goods, to mention but a few of the services which will be available to the long haul traveller from the year 2200 onwards.

*****

In the same vein the Age of Aquarius will also see some great and astonishing achievements as man realises his age-old ambition to conquer space.

In fact by the year 4000 man will occupy other planets as well as Earth.

CHAPTER SEVEN

UNIDENTIFIED FLYING OBJECTS

To those who, even in the light of the knowledge which we possess today, would suggest that man is alone in the Universe, Tall Pine and the Elders make the following reply:

"Man is arrogant and vain to even imagine that he exists alone in the Universe. The intelligence and scientific knowledge which he has so far acquired has imposed self destructive limitations upon him, to such an extent that now he is unable to think beyond that which he cannot see and touch."

The Elders assure us that there are indeed other greater and more refined minds who travel to us from afar. Those minds have in fact observed us since the primitive days when we groped around in the dark undergrowth for our prey, and sheltered from the great storms huddled together around the fire in our caves.

Some 'beings' are already here on our planet where they have been, unnoticed and undetected by man, for many years. They will make themselves known to us only when we are ready to grasp the truth. For they are visitors from another dimension, who have long since mastered the technique of travelling through the vibratory frontiers that divide their world from ours.

Our scientists, always looking anxiously outwards, towards the furthest stars for signs of life, will one day learn to explore not only deep space, but also the vibratory levels of our very own world. For we live in a multiplistic Universe in which there are worlds within worlds, each one rising in a gradually ascending scale of vibration, from the lowest to the highest.

Believe me, we are certainly not alone.

*****

In the year 2001 the UFO phenomenon will once again hit the headlines. This time some hard evidential facts will, at long last, publicly substantiate the existence of Alien craft in the Earth's airspace.

However, the concrete proof, the incontrovertible evidence of the existence of life outside our Planet, will not come until sixty to seventy years into the Millennium. At that time ' beings ' from far off planets will make indisputable contact with us, and we will come closer to actually meeting those 'beings' which have for so long been observing us from afar.

Three different kinds of Alien Beings will make their presence felt here on Earth at about the same time.

Each species will originate from a different planet, and each will have a different motive for making contact with the Earth. The intentions of two of these Alien Species will be extremely friendly towards humanity, although only one of them will show any real interest in helping the human race in any way at all.

The third group of Aliens, having made contact initially will thereafter merely observe us from a distance, seeming content to have no further communication with Earth.

However, later into the Millennium that favourite nightmare scenario of so many science fiction writers will loom as a reality over Planet Earth. For not all Alien Beings who make contact with our world in the future will do so with friendly or passive intentions towards humanity.

The major governments of the world will, out of necessity, eventually form a coalition in order to guard against invading forces from other planets. Indeed, hostile Alien forces, whose technology will be frighteningly far in advance of our own, will seek every opportunity to invade planet Earth. Unfortunately for them, though, they will be a cowardly race, and with this drawback even their superior technology will not enable them to conquer our world.

CHAPTER EIGHT

THE POPE AND RELIGION

The amazing prophecies of St Malachy which were written early in the twelfth century, all concern the Papacy.

Starting from the year 1143 he lists one hundred and twelve Popes. According to St Malachy we can expect only two more Popes before the end of the world.

St Malachy is not alone in predicting the end of the Papacy and, by inference, the end of the world. But the Elders, however, do not entirely agree here.

They tell us that four to five years into the Millennium, a new Pope will take up residence in the Vatican. In a very short time this Pope will make his radical approach to his Papal responsibilities felt. He will see it as his duty to 'clean up' in every area of the Papacy, and in attempting to do so he will refuse to be restrained or influenced by anyone.

Many Italian political bodies will begin to regard him as a threat as his influence grows and spreads.

Within seven years this Pope, who the Elders tell us will not be Italian, will die under mysterious circumstances.

Accusations of treachery and skullduggery will surround the Pope's untimely death, sparking off riots on the streets of Rome. In the fighting many people will be killed and injured.

The tragic death of this radical Pope will precipitate some extremely important and significant changes within the Catholic Church as a whole. As these changes take hold, they will spread to other leading religions.

The vow of Celibacy taken by Catholic priests will be dissolved, precipitating a division throughout the whole structure of Catholicism.

So many significant resignations will follow as a result of this bitter schism that there will be utter chaos in the hierarchy of the Catholic Church.

In my opinion the death of this Pope will mark the end of the Papacy as we know it today.

*****

In the early years of the Millennium new cults will be seen springing up all over the world as large numbers of people begin to turn away from traditional forms of religion.

The breaking down and dissolution of world religions, although a slow and gradual process, will in fact be well under way by the year 2090.

The disappearance of the established Church will leave a bitter taste in the mouths of all those who hunger and thirst for Spiritual sustenance, and it will certainly dishearten all those who have placed so much faith in traditional religions.

Throughout the first century of the new Millennium many startling revelations and scandal after scandal concerning the hierarchy of the Church will shake that institution to its very foundations.

The year 2098 is an extremely significant one for the Church. This is the year which will mark the beginning of the end for orthodox and traditional methods of worship, and of organised religion as a whole. By the year 2100 the whole concept of religion as we know it today will have been dramatically transformed, and man will have turned right back to his Pagan roots.

CHAPTER NINE

1998

SHADOWS OF THE FUTURE is due to be published at the beginning of 1998. I therefore include here a chapter of prophecies for that year. Most of them were written quite some time ago.

The majority of the ancient Seers and Prophets are generally in agreement that the years leading up to the new Millennium will be extremely significant where the evolution of mankind is concerned. In fact this period is considered by most to be a very important Spiritual Epoch, one that will reach across the entire face of Planet Earth.

As I have already mentioned elsewhere in this book Nostradamus, amongst others, prophesied that huge planetary catastrophes and violent natural disasters would bring havoc and destruction to many regions of the world in 1999. He, and others, also predicted the outbreak of great, catastrophic wars all over the planet at that time.

However, although I can see much strife and aggression breaking out throughout very many regions of the world in 1998, 'the end is certainly not nigh'.

I must say though that 1998 will most certainly be a year of worldwide aggression, famine, and major natural disasters and catastrophes.

BRITAIN 1998

1998 will be a problematic year for the Labour Government. Mr Blair will have to contend with a lot of criticism from the media and other bodies. Labour's policies, and the changes which they attempt to make, will meet with a great deal of opposition from the general public. The resignations of at least two Government Ministers will result, causing the Labour Party as a whole to be reorganised by the end of the year.

The Prime Minister himself will be the subject of criticism regarding his handling of his Government. He will be forced to make an asserted effort to win back the confidence of the British people towards the end of November 1998, but he will in fact enter 1999 under a dark cloud.

The Conservative Party, however, will enter 1999 in shining glory. They will make enormous efforts throughout the whole of 1998 to win back the affections of the British public, and by the middle of the spring of 1999 will appear to have regained the support of the country.

A new Conservative Party leader will be elected in 1998, and the leadership will appear to be making some profound and even radical changes to their policies, and to the Party as a whole.

The Labour Government will retaliate by initiating some extreme and dramatic changes to their policies, and also by managing to give the Party a whole new look.

However, right up until the end of 1998 the Prime Minister Tony Blair, and the Labour Government as a whole, will face much criticism and public outcry.

Although I see the Labour Government leading the country into the Millennium, they will certainly have a huge fight on their hands in order to do so, and radical changes will of necessity be made within the Party as a whole.

*****

Yet another IRA terrorist bombing campaign will get under way in April 1998. This one will be centred on London and Belfast.

An important 'Peace Document' will be drawn up between the British Government and representatives of the IRA. Problems ensue, however, and at the last minute the Document will NOT be signed.

Significant talks WILL take place between the British Government and IRA leaders, and steps will be taken to bring about a permanent peace in Northern Ireland. Sadly, this initiative will prove unsuccessful.

Towards the end of the year (1998) the following important discoveries will be made:

- The IRA has been responsible for a great deal more terrorist activity than was originally attributed to them
- The leaders of the IRA have been deceitful in their promises to the Irish and British people
- The IRA has received yet more finance, this time from some of the world's top powers who are sympathetic to their cause.

Following these revelations further peace proposals will only be successful for an extremely short time.

*****

1998 will begin with some terrible weather. Violent gales will sweep across the whole of Britain around the beginning of February, and many parts of the British Isles will experience freak snow storms.

The dreadful weather conditions will cause havoc and destruction, and many homes will be structurally damaged, particularly in Scotland,

Wales, and the Yorkshire Dales, these areas being particularly badly hit.

For a while driving conditions will be near impossible, and the whole of Britain will be affected by the sudden onset of freezing temperatures which will cause the deaths, in one way or another, of many people.

Although the summer of 1998 will be one of the hottest for many years, there will be a price to pay, as it will bring with it unexpected torrential rains and thunderstorms.

There will be an extremely hot Indian Summer, right through until the late autumn, which will be followed by one of the coldest and most chilling winters for many years. The British Isles will once again be thrown into veritable chaos. Gales and rainstorms will sweep the country.

By the start of 1999 Britain will be beginning to accept the dramatic transformation in its weather. The summer of 1999 will be the longest and hottest on record.

*****

1998 will most certainly be yet another problematic year for the Royal Family.

Early in the year some startling suggestions will be made public about the death of Diana, Princess of Wales. As a result, the Prime Minister will have a meeting with the Queen. The results of this meeting will be made public, and the Prime Minister will subsequently address the British nation on television, in an attempt to quell the fears and anxieties felt by so many people concerning Diana's death.

Much later on in the year more revelations on this subject will surface, and will be made public.

Towards the end of 1998 there will be another meeting between the Queen and the Prime Minister, but this meeting will concern the future of the Royal Family, and will be held as a result of mounting criticism of them from the general public, and in the media.

1998 will be another difficult year for Prince Charles. Throughout March, April and May he will find himself under constant attack from several quarters concerning his treatment of Diana.

Charles will visit the USA later on in the year in an attempt to win the confidence and affection of the American people. He will also become actively involved in more and more of Diana's unfinished work.

Illness will strike the Royal Family in 1998 when the Queen Mother is taken ill and admitted to hospital. Her failing health will cause concern. However, she will make a full recovery, although later on in the year she will develop a respiratory condition.

Towards the end of 1998 Prince Edward and his fiance will be in the news.

*****

In 1998 a particularly horrible crime will hit the headlines all over the country.

During the robbery of a north London National Westminster Bank someone will be shot and killed.

*****

In the month of November 1998 there will be a catastrophe at sea. Several people will be killed.

In the same month an air disaster will only just be avoided when two planes narrowly miss colliding with each other in mid air in the vicinity of London.

*****

The entertainer Danny La Rue, and the veteran film star Sir Richard Attenborough will both be in the news in 1998.

The world of entertainment, and the British public, will be saddened by the sudden death of a much loved celebrity.

The international movie world will mourn the death of a 1950s star of musicals.

*****

Towards the end of 1998 a well respected, veteran Political figure will die suddenly.

The Liverpool band SPACE, with its talented song writer and bass guitarist Tommy Scott, will rise suddenly to national fame and popularity in late 1998, following the release of their new album, which will be an instant success.

IRAQ 1998

Iraq will once again be a hot bed of friction in 1998.

Up until the month of April the trouble there will be fairly low key. However, the situation will reach a crescendo around the beginning of June, when the aggression exhibited by the Iraqis will attract interest from various

53

major world bodies.

Although the trouble will appear to die down somewhat around mid July, the Western world will merely have been lulled into a false sense of security. Fighting will break out once again when Iraq's aggression explodes once more.

There will be trouble in this area throughout the summer months and into the early autumn. At this time American and British organisations will unite in a show of strength and power against Iraq, in order to prevent a further escalation of the situation.

AUSTRALIA 1998

Towards the end of July or the beginning of August 1998 parts of Australia will be seriously affected when a disastrous earthquake occurs, causing havoc and destruction.

The horror of this earthquake will be followed by some very unseasonal, unpredictable, bad weather, and a hurricane will actually sweep across Australia in late summer, laying waste homes, buildings and land.

As if this were not enough, further turbulent weather will follow.

HONG KONG 1998

The first signs of the imminent approach of a really problematic time in Hong Kong will emerge in 1998.

The Chinese government will begin to impose great restrictions on the people of Hong Kong, and towards the end of 1998 they will make an announcement to the Western world concerning the future of the former colony.

ISRAEL 1998

There will be a great deal of friction and aggression in Israel and in the Arab States during 1998.

Many people will die as a result of terrorist activity there.

A leading Israeli public figure will be assassinated.

The ensuing turmoil and strife will necessitate the intervention of other major international powers, in the interests of world peace.

RUSSIA 1998

An important Russian figure will die suddenly in 1998, and the country will be plunged into veritable chaos for a very short period, during which governmental adjustments will be made.

The British Prime Minister will visit Russia following the sudden death.

GERMANY 1998

1998 will see the beginning of strife in parts of Germany. Trouble will break out in colleges and Universities all over the country, organised and precipitated by a neo Nazi political Party

Chaos will reign, and although the government will regain control of the situation, no real solution will be found.

USA 1998

In July and August 1998 there will be two major air disasters involving American and British planes. These disasters will result in the deaths of all those involved.

MEDICINE 1998

An extremely significant breakthrough will be made in the treatment of one of the worst forms of cancer.

Although this treatment will be only in its early stages, the news of the breakthrough will herald the coming of the end of one of the most dreaded diseases.

Later on in 1998 there will be yet another breakthrough, this time in the relief of spinal injuries and pain. Although also in its innovative stages, the treatment will be a highly important breakthrough in the relief of these debilitating conditions.

CHAPTER TEN

AN OVERVIEW

Most schools of Esoteric thought agree that each 'AGE' lasts for approximately 2100 years and that we are, at the present time, just moving out of the AGE OF PISCES into the NEW AGE of AQUARIUS.

The Elders, however, tell us that not only did the AGE OF AQUARIUS begin around the mid 1960s, but that it will last only approximately 1890 years, at which time we will begin to see the emergence of the exciting AGE OF CAPRICORN.

The advent in the 1960s of the Age of Aquarius was marked by a sudden and widespread interest in the ecology of the planet. This interest in the welfare of Planet Earth and all who exist upon her has now become an integral part of the school curriculum. As a result, the youth of today are certainly much more 'Planet Conscious' than ever before, and are leading the way in the fight for conservation, animal rights, and a cleaner, pollutant free Earth.

However, the Age of Aquarius does in fact require a 'settling in' period, and this is likely to last another seventy years or so. During this time ANYTHING can happen on the planet and, the Elders assure us, a great deal WILL.

There will be an enormous amount of discord and strife in many Eastern countries over the next sixty to seventy years. There will be some extremely volatile situations, involving the threat of warfare.

Seventy years into the Millennium and beyond this discord will gradually shift to the Western regions of the planet.

The imminent and absolute end of the world, brought about either by some huge natural disaster, or by man's shameful ignorance in a destructive world war which would wipe out humanity and leave planet Earth uninhabitable, does not figure as such in the prophecies of the Elders.

On the contrary, I am given to understand that for the future of mankind there is only change, transmutation and growth. Nonetheless, the Elders DO say that things must get markedly worse before they get better, and I am certain that where the future of our planet is concerned, this will definitely be the case.

Ninety years into the Millennium the world will be brought to its knees by a disastrous world war, which will come close to fulfilling all those gloom and doom prophecies from the past.

But mankind will struggle through this darkest of hours, and life will go on.

I feel that here is perhaps an appropriate moment at which to mention the plight of the Animal Kingdom. Throughout all the ages the animals of this planet have sustained the human race. They have evolved alongside us, but are powerless to stop man's systematic destruction of their habitats. So spare a thought for those who cannot shape their own destiny, for humanity simply could not survive in a world devoid of animal life.

Two hundred years into the Millennium the world will once again be a hot bed of friction and discord. Although stopping short of outright war, major countries will attempt to assert their power over others, while smaller countries will be struggling for their continued existence.

Over and above man's inhumanity and ignorance planetary disasters, such as volcanic eruptions and earthquakes, will abound. It will almost seem at that time as though the planet herself has had enough of the ignorant race which has for so long abused her.

However, throughout all the suffering mankind has already endured, and will in the future endure, life will continue.

By this time, around the year 2200, normal human life expectancy will have risen to approximately one hundred and fifty , and in some cases two hundred years, as new discoveries and inventions make life much more comfortable for the elderly and disabled.

Two hundred years into the Millennium the human form will have evolved to such an extent that the average height for a male will be approximately 7.5 to 8 feet. The female height will be slightly less, with an average of 7.2 to 7.10 feet. The future, it would seem, will breed a world of veritable giants!

On the other hand, medical science will at this time be struggling to eradicate terrible diseases, some which we have never known before, and some which will be 'new' forms of ancient diseases.

The Elders tell us that the Age of Aquarius is a vital Age of 'preparation', during which mankind must make ready for the dawning of the Age of Capricorn.

Although the 1960s was an important Spiritual Epoch, it was in fact only the preparation period for the Epoch that is to come with the approaching Millennium. The Elders refer to this Epoch as 'THE GOLDEN AGE OF SPIRIT'.

This Golden Age will begin in earnest two hundred and twenty five years into the Millennium, and will gain strength throughout the rest of the Age of Aquarius.

The dawning of the following Age, that of Capricorn, will usher in a Spiritual Revolution upon the Earth - the long awaited planetary awakening. The strong family influences of Capricorn will unite mankind in their endeavours to promote peace and harmony throughout the world.

Man will finally learn to live and work together.

Sadly, though, the Age of Capricorn will also unite mankind in their efforts to combat the elements. For the Earth's climate, already by this time almost unrecognisable from the climate of today, will change even more.

Great disasters will be experienced all over the planet during the Age of Capricorn - land masses will disappear, submerged beneath the rising waters of the Oceans; violently erupting volcanoes will lay waste miles of land around them; torrential rains will cause disastrous flooding, and strong, drying winds will cause fertile regions to become arid wastelands.

Although there will still be a lot of land visible on the planet at this time, some of it will have been rendered uninhabitable due to volcanic activity or adverse climatic conditions. Earthquakes will have opened up enormous fissures in the earth, from which great fires will blaze, ignited and fuelled by naturally evolved gases.

These phenomena will be seen all over the planet, some areas of which will resemble the more morbid scenes from today's science fiction movies.

*****

There are those who would say, even today, that 'Big Business' wields too much influence in governmental affairs.

Do we really want the interests of Big Business to influence government policy? they ask. What happens to impartiality, they cry, when money changes hands?

The Elders tell us that there will be NO lessening of the power and influence of business and industry in the future. In fact it will greatly increase, and two hundred years into the new Millennium we will begin to see the virtual 'sponsorship' of governments by Business.

Eventually governments as such will become redundant, they will be powerless bodies, dominated by vast business enterprises.

The snowball effect of the growth of the influence of Business over governments across the world will culminate, by the year 3000, in the establishment of one major planetary 'GOVERNING COUNCIL'. This Governing Council will have its headquarters in Canada.

Today most of us would regard the possibility of this sort of World Government with alarm, fearing that it could only bring chaos to the world. However, nothing could be further from the truth. For the Elders tell us that the establishment of this Governing Council for the whole Earth will establish global peace, once and for all.

58

By the year 4300 huge crafts will be built on water, large enough to accommodate thousands of people. The future will see floating man-made islands, some of which will be constructed under glass domes to protect the inhabitants from the elements.

Life in our world in the far future will be very different from the life we know here today. But by this time mankind will have made such scientific progress that accessible planets in our solar system, capable of maintaining human life, will already have been discovered.

One day man will, by necessity, leave Planet Earth behind.

*****

Contrary to popular belief, and to the stuff of science fiction, the Moon will never be inhabitable. However, great observation posts will be erected there, and it will be used as a convenient storage area, far enough away from Earth for some undesirable or dangerous substances or machinery to be kept.

*****

It is true to say that no one knows exactly why Avatars, Enchristed Ones, are born, and why indeed they are chosen to be Avatars. Perhaps it is that they come in response to the collective cries and prayers of the masses.

Whatever the reason we can be quite certain that the new Millennium, and the approaching Golden Age, will truly bring about the re emergence of the Masters and Sages of old.

Looking back throughout history we can see that the Earth has passed through periods which marked specific and profound changes in the moral, ethical, and Spiritual attitudes of mankind. We might call these periods 'Times of Spiritual Transformation'.

Such will be the coming GOLDEN AGE.

In the same way, when looking back we can identify periods in history during which mankind has Spiritually deteriorated, falling into a sort of dark period of debauchery, crime, and evil. Once a country or nation has known such evil and depravity it has the greatest difficulty in freeing itself from the shadows cast by such dark experiences. It is never enough to educate and thereby cleanse the minds of the people, for it is necessary too to cleanse the very Spiritual air they breathe, and the very space through which they walk.

This cleansing will only come about with the passing of time, and the evolutionary processes of the collective consciousness of the masses.

But even then, the psychic space of that nation may, for hundreds of years after, remain charged with those dark, evil energies discharged and set in motion by their demonic perpetrators, which will reach out to and influence the minds of all those who live there.

Mankind would do well to remember that thoughts are truly living things.

So the coming Millennium will once again bear witness to that age old struggle of Good versus Evil, with the advent of the Anti Christ and the re emergence of the Avatars. It will at times appear as though the very end of Creation is at hand, as man struggles through the black clouds of destruction and pestilence.

But the Golden Age of Spirit is beckoning, and the Spiritual natures of man are collectively quickening. Mankind's Spiritual liberation awaits, in the bright sunshine beyond the looming Shadows of the Future.

CHAPTER ELEVEN

QUESTIONS AND ANSWERS

In this chapter Tall Pine answers some frequently asked, relevant questions.

Q. WHAT EXACTLY IS THE 'SPIRIT' OR THE 'REAL SELF'?

A. The physical body and the mind of man combined constitute the personality or the lesser self, and merely represent the Spiritual Essence on the physical level.

The Real or Eternal Self, whose manifestation is in individuality, is truly indestructible, and certainly cannot in any way die. Even when the physical body has decayed and disintegrated the Spirit still lives on, simply because nothing can kill or destroy it - it cannot die.

It is like a circle, it has no beginning and no end.

The highest manifestations of man's being are often seen to be expressed through his creative abilities, and sometimes through the courage he exhibits in the face of adversity, danger, or even life threatening illness. A weak man can find great strength when he most needs it, and can astound others with his achievements as he unleashes an unexpected burst of power.

The weak man can most certainly conquer the strong man, sometimes by sheer cunning, but often by exhibiting a strength which obviously has nothing whatsoever to do with his physical stature.

Q. DOES PLANET EARTH POSSESS A SPIRIT?

A. Of course. The Earth itself is a living organism capable of feeling, thinking, seeing and knowing. The whole of the planet upon which you live and have your being is alive with Spiritual energy, pulsating through and manifesting in the beauty of Nature. The magnificent display of colour that washes across each seasonal scene; the birds whistling and singing like some strange enchanted symphony sounding in some far off world; the eagle soaring on the morning breeze; the trees rustling in the wind, and the movement of the grass across the winter meadow. The moving river, the mountains that sleep, the sunrise and the dawn. Need I say more? All this is an exhibition and manifestation of the SPIRIT OF THE EARTH.

Q. WILL THE DAY EVER DAWN WHEN THE EARTH TIRES OF THE WAY IN WHICH MAN ABUSES HER? IF SO, WHAT WILL SHE DO?

A. She will respond as anyone who is abused or cruelly treated would do - she will retaliate. But this is not what she is presently doing, no, she is not presently responding to your mistreatment of her.

The Earth has been raped and abused. Man has taken from her without replacing what he has taken. He has been thoughtless, he has polluted the waters of the lakes, rivers and Oceans. In turn he is destroying the thin atmosphere, that which man calls Ozone, around the Earth.

But Mother Earth knows full well that she need do nothing at all. For man is punishing himself by his own actions. He is destroying the Earth, and in so doing he is destroying himself. Are not the seasons turning upon him, and the Black Wolves of disease devouring him?

Man must dramatically transform the way he thinks of Nature and the Great Universe. Then, and only then, shall these transform the way they think of him.

Q. SOME OF THE THINGS YOU HAVE ALREADY PROPHE-SIED ARE QUITE FRIGHTENING, AND OTHER THINGS ARE EXCITING. HOW IS IT THAT YOU ARE ABLE TO SEE ALL THOSE THINGS IN THE FUTURE SO CLEARLY? AND IS IT POSSIBLE TO CHANGE OUR FUTURE?

A. Think of me as standing on the peak of the highest mountain. As I look down at you I can see all those things coming towards you, and all those things which have already passed you by.

In reality I exist in a timeless, abstract world in which all those things that have been, and all those things which are yet to be, coexist in an eternal moment, unencumbered by the limitations of man's ephemeral mind. It is all that man can do to perceive his life from a backward view, when all that he desires to know of his future is spread out on the horizon before him, like the landscape of an unknown land.

But you see, your future has already taken wings, and presently flaps around you like the wings of an invisible bird across the waters of a great ocean.

No. Your future cannot be changed.

Q. WILL MORE USE BE MADE OF PSYCHICS IN THE FUTURE, AND WILL THE ABILITIES OF SUCH PEOPLE BE MORE POWERFUL THAN THEY ARE TODAY?

A. Most certainly. It is known that before man evolved speech as a mode of communication he used what you call 'Telepathy' as a means of expressing his thoughts and feelings. This ability has long since been lost to man because of the way in which his world has evolved, making his life much easier. Consequently there is now no necessity for him to use

Telepathy in his everyday life.

However, the approaching Millennium will give birth to extremely gifted children whose abilities will be astonishing, causing your scientists to rethink their theories about TIME and SPACE and THE UNIVERSE.

Even today there are children born who shall, in due course, exhibit extraordinary metaphysical powers, and who shall work hand in hand with your scientists.

The mind of man is capable of creating incredible powers, powers which can in turn create or destroy. The day will come when the only weapons used in your needless and senseless wars will be the powers of the mind.

Within you there is more.

CHAPTER TWELVE

CONCLUSION

I have often been asked to explain exactly how I receive the prophecies. It is usually assumed that I have to enter a 'trance-like state' in order to do so.

The various ways in which the Elders communicate their thoughts, and the methods which they use to do so, have long been a source of fascination to me. There does not appear to be any set pattern.

I have certainly never been able to command communication from the Elders. Wasn't it Byron who once said of poetry

"Poetry is a distinct faculty - it won't come when called - you may as well whistle for the wind".

Lord Byron's view sums up my contact with the Elders perfectly for, try as I may, I cannot at any time call them to me, I can merely send them a mental request. Should there be no response to my request there is absolutely nothing I can do.

Communication usually takes place in the evening when, I suppose, I am feeling more relaxed. I have noticed that before the communications occur I become extremely sleepy, and remain so for twenty minutes or more. After that time I feel myself become anxious, even agitated, and experience an overwhelming need to walk around the room.

Then, once I have settled myself into a comfortable position I gradually become aware of the 'Controlling Entity', which is usually, although not always, Tall Pine.

A feeling of total peace descends on me and I become oblivious to everything, remaining in this state until the communications have been completed.

Most often, as far as I am aware, the prophecies are dictated to me by a clear articulate voice, sounding not at all as one would expect a North American Indian to sound.

At other times I may receive the communications as extraneous thoughts, depending on who the communicator is.

It is easy to understand why many of the ancient Seers used a mixture of herbal narcotics and alcohol to bring about a self induced trance-like stupor, thereby quickening the process wherein they received prophetic visions. In this way the prophecies would have been under their control. Most of their prophetic visions, and here Nostradamus is a prime example, were purely the results of their abilities to project themselves mentally into an 'Astral State', albeit under the influence of some narcotic substance.

In my case, although I also enter an 'Astral State', I am in fact totally dependent upon the discarnate members of the Elders for the prophecies. As I have already said, should they choose not to communicate with me for any reason, there is absolutely nothing I can do about it.

Although I have been receiving teachings from the Elders for more than twenty five years, I do not for one moment assume that I have the monopoly upon them and their work. The Elders, I believe, are dedicated to the propagation of Spiritual Truths and to the Spiritual Evolution of mankind. They place a great deal of emphasis on meditation, and teach that through it man is capable of greater and more profound things.

One of the Elders, an Oriental gentleman known to me only as Golden Moon, appears to play an extremely important part in the prophetic communications, imparting them to me mainly in dreams.

Some of the more startling revelations in this book were in fact channelled some years ago and have been gathering dust on a lonely shelf until now, when I feel the right time has come for them to see the light of day.

READ BILLY ROBERTS

Billy Roberts writes for the monthly paper Psychic World. If you would like to read his monthly column then see below.

P S Y C H I C   W O R L D

Psychic World is the monthly paper that covers a wide variety of topics. Covering Spiritualism, the paranormal, news, E.V.P., scientific aspects of Spiritualism, philosophy, views and other subjects.

Our writers include editor **Ray Taylor BA.**, assistant editor **Michael Colmer, Matthew Hutton** book reviews, Science **Ron Pearson, Michael Roll**, New age **Dave Robinson** also **Billy Roberts**, from the U.S.A. **Gary Williams, Al Collier** and from Australia **Dr Nassif Isaac**, etc.

Why not join the growing band of readers of **Psychic World**?
For subscription details send S.A.E. to:-

Psychic World Publishing Company Limited, P.O. Box 14, Greenford, Middlesex, UB6 0UF.